Original title:
Elfin Laughter on Christmas Night

Copyright © 2024 Creative Arts Management OÜ
All rights reserved.

Author: Nolan Kingsley
ISBN HARDBACK: 978-9916-90-908-9
ISBN PAPERBACK: 978-9916-90-909-6

Frosty Chats in Twilight's Hold

In the stillness, snowflakes race,
Chasing squirrels in a frosty space.
Frogs in scarves, they leap and croak,
Sharing jokes with a friendly oak.

Bouncing snowballs for a good laugh,
While penguins play a game of half.
Hot cocoa spills, the cups take flight,
As winter holds the day so tight.

Midnight Whispers of Joyful Spirits

Moonbeams dance on melting ice,
Elves in pajamas, isn't that nice?
Ticklish icicles laugh and sway,
While gnomes tell tales of their wild play.

Jingle bells ring with a cheerful thud,
A snowman trips, covered in mud.
Ghosts in coats, with whiskers a-flare,
Share secrets of desserts beyond compare.

Revelries Beneath the Snowy Blanket

Winter critters throw a grand bash,
With a snowball fight that's quite the clash.
Bears in mittens sip frozen gin,
While chickens dance a raucous spin.

Marshmallow candies stack up high,
The raccoons joke, "Look at the sky!"
With laughter echoing through the night,
As snowflakes wink with chilly delight.

Frosted Delight in a Starry Serenade

Starlit skies above the trees,
Fill the night with giggles and pleas.
Bumblebees wear tiny boots,
Dancing on tops of snowy roots.

A frosty cake with sparkles bright,
Served by owls in sheer delight.
Joyful whispers as snowflakes glide,
In this magic, we all reside.

The Dance of the Woodland Whimsy

In the glen where the shadows play,
Squirrels twirl, chasing the day.
With acorns high, they leap and bound,
Making mischief without a sound.

A badger dons a top hat tight,
While rabbits waltz in pure delight.
They trip and slip on muddy ground,
With giggles ringing all around.

Jingles of Enchantment in the Air

The wind hums soft with a jolly tune,
While frogs hold court beneath the moon.
Tiny fairies join the jive,
Spinning dreams that come alive.

A plump old owl hoots a beat,
While mice tap dance with tiny feet.
Nectar sipped from daisy cups,
As giggles and laughter bubble up.

Secrets of the Celestial Merry-Makers

Stars twinkle bright with secret glee,
As comets swirl like birds set free.
A moonbeam winks in silver light,
Whispering tales of frolic and flight.

Cosmic critters in a stellar scuffle,
Tumble through space with joyous chuckle.
They trade sweet notes with sugar clouds,
As laughter echo through cosmic crowds.

Fables of Frost and Cheer

Snowflakes fall, a frosty dance,
While penguins waddle in a trance.
Each flake a tale from winter's quill,
Of giggles shared on the snowy hill.

A snowman laughs with a carrot nose,
As twinkling lights put on a show.
With every toss of snowball cheer,
Winter's magic spreads far and near.

Nighttime Revelers in the Glimmering Wood

In the forest, shadows dance,
A squirrel's joke leads to a prance.
Owls with spectacles take their seats,
Listening close to the night's fun tweets.

Fireflies flash their tiny lights,
Critters gather for giggly nights.
Rabbits hop in a conga line,
While raccoons sip on berry wine.

Chipmunks wear their tiny hats,
Telling tales of old, silly spats.
The moonbeams laugh at the scene,
As the woods fill with joyful sheen.

So if you hear a burst of cheer,
Just know the night is filled with beer.
Join the fun in the glimmering wood,
Where laughter thrives, and all is good!

Shimmering Laughter Among the Pines

In pines so tall, the giggles soar,
As squirrels juggle acorns galore.
A raccoon cracks a nutty joke,
And laughter echoes through each oak.

Beneath the stars, a dance takes flight,
With bunnies spinning left and right.
A fox in shades struts with pride,
While hedgehogs cheer from the side.

The breeze brings whispers, soft delight,
As night critters revel in the light.
They toast to friendship, wild and sweet,
With berry punch and honeyed treats.

So join the fun with woodland friends,
Where laughter starts and never ends.
Among the pines, a joyous spree,
In shimmering laughter, wild and free!

Jingle Bells and Enchanted Swells

With Santa hats and jingles bright,
The critters gather in the night.
A badger croons a funny tune,
While raccoons dance under the moon.

Jingle bells clink on their tails,
As they set sail on snowy trails.
Penguins slide with gleeful spins,
And a hedgehog just can't stop his grins.

Eggnog flows from mushrooms tall,
As everyone is having a ball.
The chill in the air can't freeze their cheer,
For laughter warms each furry ear.

So raise a cup to festive spells,
In a woodland where joy compels.
With jingle bells and enchanted swells,
Join the merry, can't you tell?

Starlight Frolics and Cheerful Mirth

Underneath the starlit skies,
Come the woodland pals in disguise.
Dancing deer with glittering shoes,
And playful owls with colorful hues.

The frogs croak out a silly beat,
As badgers stomp their furry feet.
A raccoon spins a funky tale,
While nightingales join in the wail.

Laughter bubbles in every nook,
As the night unfolds like a book.
Tales of mischief and of cheer,
Fill the air with warmth and beer.

So if you wander through the park,
Join the fun, don't be a lark.
With starlight frolics and mirth so bright,
You'll find your heart feels just right!

Pinecone Mischiefs and Jolly Secrets

Pinecones bouncing on the ground,
A squirrel's laughter all around.
He thinks he's clever, oh so sly,
But slips and lands right on a pie!

Jolly secrets whispered low,
Where pine trees dance and breezes blow.
A mischievous chipmunk runs with glee,
While acorns sing, "Come climb with me!"

The Snowfall's Silly Serenade

Snowflakes tumble, one, two, three,
A snowman grins, oh what a spree!
With buttons made from juicy fruit,
   He steals a carrot, what a hoot!

Snowball fights erupt with cheer,
As penguins slide, no hint of fear.
A puppy leaps into the air,
While snowmen giggle everywhere!

Frosty Frolics and Starlit Yonder

The frost is nippy, chill is bright,
But frosty fun brings sheer delight.
With scarves that swirl, the children play,
Creating laughter through the gray!

Under the stars, they dance and prance,
In twinkling shoes, they take a chance.
Frosty kisses in the night,
The moon beams down, all feels just right.

The Spritely Joy Beneath the Boughs

Beneath the boughs where shadows creep,
A rabbit plays while the squirrels sleep.
With hops and skips, he makes a mess,
As fallen leaves become his dress!

The flowers giggle, the bees agree,
The best of fun is wild and free.
A joyful dance through all the green,
Life's funny moments, a happy scene!

Whispers of Frost Under Starlit Skies

Beneath the moon, a snowman grins,
His carrot nose, a source of sins.
A scarf too long, it wraps around,
He tripped and fell without a sound.

The chilly breeze begins to tease,
While penguins dance with utmost ease.
They waddle close, and one does slip,
And now he needs a winter trip!

The stars up high, they shimmer bright,
While squirrels plan their midnight flight.
They race with snowflakes in a spin,
And all the trees join in with grins.

So gather 'round, let's share a laugh,
At frosty jokes and snowy craft.
For in this chill where giggles rise,
We find warm hearts beneath the skies.

Mirth of the Winter Sprites

The winter sprites, they sit and scheme,
With snowflakes soft, they plot and dream.
They hide in gloves and peek in hats,
    And sprinkle joy like furry cats.

A tumble here, a giggle there,
They sprinkle snow in folks' own hair.
A snowball flies, a squeal is heard,
    As laughter bubbles, stirs the herd!

With mugs of cocoa piled with cream,
They swap their tales and plot's supreme.
A snowman's dance turns quite absurd,
    Each jig and poke makes laughter stir.

So if you hear a giggly sound,
Look close and see what's all around.
For winter sprites are full of cheer,
    And spread their joy from far to near.

Twilight Giggles in the Snow

As twilight falls, the snowflakes twirl,
A frosty dance, a cozy whirl.
The bunnies hop, their tails a blur,
While cheeky kids toss snow with slur.

The shadows stretch, a funny sight,
Snowmen chatting, hearts delight.
They whisper jokes with frosty breath,
Of carrots gone and winter's wealth.

The candles flicker, warm and bright,
While snowball fights bring pure delight.
Giggles bounce through the frosty land,
As we embrace this snowy band.

So let us laugh, let warmth ignite,
In winter's chill, our hearts feel light.
For twilight giggles snowflakes bring,
A merry tune for all to sing.

Glistening Shadows of Joyful Spirits

In winter's hush, the shadows dance,
Happy spirits in a trance.
They twirl through snow, with glee they glide,
Each gleaming spark a winking ride.

The stars above watch close and wink,
While snowmen sip their cups and drink.
A comet smiles, a reindeer prances,
In winter's chill, the magic enhances.

With giggles rising, spirits soar,
Each fallen flake unlocks the door.
To laughter bright, to joy unbound,
In frosty realms, sweet joys are found.

So join the dance, let shadows play,
In glistening light, we'll find our way.
For joyful spirits love to tease,
Creating smiles with every breeze.

Giddy Snowflakes on Merry Winds

Snowflakes twirl with glee and dance,
Spinning 'round in frosty pants.
They tumble down like quirky sprites,
Landing soft on noses bright.

Snowmen grin with carrot flair,
Frosty hats and lopsided hair.
They come alive with silly cheer,
And up they throw their snowball beer!

Sleds go zooming down the hills,
With squeals of laughter, all the thrills.
Hot cocoa drips upon our chins,
We can't stop grinning, let the fun begin!

So as the winter wraps its cloak,
Let's giggle loud, and let's all joke.
With giddy snowflakes in the air,
We'll cherish every flake and dare!

Mirth in the Mesmerizing Dark

Night falls softly, stars ignite,
Crickets chirp their songs of light.
Ghosts in blankets, peek and play,
Just don't let them lead you astray.

Bats in capes fly overhead,
Whispering secrets from their bed.
The moon winks down, a big white grin,
Shhh! There's a party, let it begin!

Owls throw hats and dance in trees,
While shadows sway like gallant bees.
With every rustle, giggles grow,
In the dark, let mirth overflow!

So gather close, and don't you fret,
The night holds joy, and not regret.
In this whimsical twilight spree,
We'll laugh and dance - oh, can't you see?

Silvery Shadows with Glowing Grins

Shadows creep with playful glee,
They giggle low, just wait and see.
With glimmering eyes, they leap and glide,
Living in laughter, what a ride!

Ghostly figures, jests galore,
They whisper tales of yore and more.
In moonlit corners, they convene,
Cackling sharply, like a dream!

Spooky snacks and phantom drinks,
Join the feast while everyone winks.
No spooky scares, just goofy sights,
In this delightful ghostly night!

So let's dance with shadows bold,
In their warm embrace, we'll never feel cold.
With glowing grins and silly charms,
We'll hold each other in joyful arms!

Hearthside Tales of Playful Times

By the fire, tales are spun,
Of silly antics, laughter's fun.
A cat named Mr. Wiggly Paw,
Could make a moose jump with a flaw.

The cookies burn while laughter snorts,
As grandmas share their funny sorts.
'Back in my day!' they start to say,
In giggles lost, they drift away.

With mugs of soup and wobbly chairs,
Each story weaves through playful airs.
The hearth glows bright, the spirits soar,
In this coziness, we all adore!

So gather round, all hearts align,
In hearthside tales, our joy will shine.
Playful times and laughter's bliss,
Are moments we will surely miss!

Yule Revelry's Mischievous Echo

In a land of snowflakes, twinkling bright,
Santa's reindeer took a flight.
They played hide and seek through the trees,
While elves giggled, doing as they please.

A snowman danced with a candy cane,
His top hat tipped, causing him pain.
He slipped on ice, what a sight,
As carolers laughed with pure delight.

Gifts under the tree, all wrapped so tight,
But one box sneezed, Oh what a fright!
It popped open, confetti flew,
Now everyone's wearing a silly shoe!

Yule logs burn while cookies bake,
But the cat just made a big mistake.
He jumped for joy, then fell in the pie,
Now who will rescue him? Oh my, oh my!

Twinkling Tinsel and Sassy Grins

Tinsel sparkles with a cheeky flair,
While grandma tries to fix her hair.
The tree's a sight, with lights aglow,
But the cat thinks it's fair game, you know!

Ornaments hang like a wild parade,
One's a pirate, the other, a spade.
The kids giggle and point with glee,
As the dog snags a snack under the tree.

Fluffy snowflakes fall, they swirl and spin,
But watch your head, here comes a grin!
Snowballs fly, with laughter too,
They all land smack on Dad's shiny shoe.

With warm cocoa, the night takes flight,
As shadows dance in the moonlight.
The fun rolls on, like a merry tune,
On this jolly night, we'll party till noon!

Midnight Magic in Enchanted Woods

Beneath the moon, the fairies play,
Making wishes on a glitter ray.
A gnome nearby, with a crooked hat,
Tries to dance but falls—how about that?

Trees are giggling, branches sway,
While pixies toast their drinks of hay.
A squirrel juggles acorns with flair,
Oh, what a sight to behold out there!

Mischief abounds in the midnight air,
As owls hoot and sing without a care.
The woodland critters join in the fun,
Dancing and prancing, they never run!

As dawn approaches, colors ignite,
With whispers of magic, they take flight.
The woods are lively, laughter's the key,
In this enchanted place where we're all free!

Giggling Sprites in Snowy Dreams

In the land of snow and endless cheer,
Giggling sprites swirl without a fear.
They twirl and toss snowflakes galore,
Belly laughs echo, who could ask for more?

With tiny bells that jingle and chime,
They sneak and peek—oh, what a crime!
They steal a nibble from hot pies,
And leave behind giggles with surprise!

The moonlight sparkles on snowy hills,
While the sprites prank with their giggly thrills.
They hide in bushes, they pop out quick,
Ghosting the kids with a playful trick!

Dreams of snowmen and candy canes,
Whispers of laughter in frosty lanes.
In winter's wonder, they frolic and gleam,
Oh, what a joy—this snowy dream!

Festive Whimsy in the Chilling Air

Snowmen with hats on their heads,
Dance in the yard while kids hide in beds.
With carrot-noses that wobble and sway,
They'll challenge the sun for a warm winter's day.

Hot cocoa spills down mugs with glee,
Marshmallows afloat like tiny boats at sea.
Elves, with their giggles, bring cheer all around,
And the jingle of bells is the sweetest of sounds.

Icicles hang like teeth on display,
As squirrels throw snowball battles in play.
Frosty the Snowman run, don't you trip!
You're meant to be merry, not take a cold dip.

While snowflakes fall like glitter from the sky,
We build festive forts, oh my, oh my!
The chill in the air just adds to the fun,
With laughter and mischief until day is done.

Enchanted Laughter of the Winter Fairies

In the moonlight glow, fairies do twirl,
Spreading dust and giggles with every swirl.
They tickle the noses of sleepyhead bears,
And play peek-a-boo with snowflakes in pairs.

With mischievous grins, they ride on a breeze,
Twirling through trees like they own the leaves.
They sprinkle their laughter, a magical sound,
Turning the forest into joy all around.

Their wings made of frost, light as a sigh,
They giggle and nibble on pie from the sky.
When winter's chill dawns and blankets the land,
These fairies bring warmth with their whimsical band.

So if you find footprints in fresh snowy fields,
Look closely for giggles, their charm never yields.
For laughter is magic that glows in the cold,
And winter's bright fairies bring stories untold.

Riddles Wrapped in Sparkling Light

On a shimmering night, the stars twist and spin,
With riddles of wonder, let the fun begin.
What has keys but can't open a door?
A piano, you say, oh, we need more!

Wrapped in twinkling lights, the trees stand tall,
Whispers of secrets they share with us all.
What runs around town but never moves fast?
Little snowballs that cover the grass!

The moon grins down, a big cheese in the sky,
As snowflakes float gently, making all spirits fly.
What's a snowman's favorite drink, I wonder?
Ice tea of course, a cute little blunder!

As riddles unfold, laughter fills the air,
In this sparkling night, let's spread joy everywhere.
For every giggle can melt any fear,
And riddles wrapped in light bring loved ones near.

Candy-Cane Dreams and Brightened Minds

Candy-cane dreams dance in sugar-filled skies,
With peppermint whispers that tickle our eyes.
Jingle bells jangle, it's a sweet little sound,
As children make wishes where joy can be found.

Gingerbread houses line streets made of fluff,
With icing on rooftops, it's all quite enough.
What do you call a snowman with a six-pack?
An abdominal snowman! It's a silly hack!

From twinkling of lights to the smell of good cheer,
The magic of winter draws family near.
What's Santa's favorite type of music style?
Wrap music is great for a holiday smile!

With laughter like snowflakes, each one unique,
We share all our secrets with a giggle and squeak.
In candy-cane dreams, our hearts soar and swell,
For the gift of good times is the best treat of all.

Frosty Pixies' Tender Rhymes

In the chilly night, they dance with glee,
They twirl and spin, as happy as can be.
With snowflakes in hair, and a giggle so bright,
Frosty pixies play till the morning light.

They poke fun at icicles, oh what a sight!
Slippery little things, they slip in delight.
"Watch out!" they yell, with a wink and a cheer,
As snowmen melt down, it's their time of year.

Chubby cheeks glow, cheeks all aglow,
While frost-covered trees wear a shimmering show.
With candy cane wands, they tickle and tease,
The giggles erupt, dancing on the breeze.

So let's join the fun, forget winter's chill,
With frosty pixies, there's laughter to spill.
In the land of the snow, joy beams in their eyes,
For each frosty night holds mysterious surprise.

Glistening Laughter of the Winter Spirits

Snowflakes are falling, like laughter in air,
Winter spirits giggle, spreading joy everywhere.
With snowmen and angels, they play in the drifts,
Each joke crafted carefully, their best little gifts.

They slide down the slopes, on slushy old trays,
With bright-colored scarves, they weave through the haze.
"Catch me if you can!" they holler with glee,
As they dodge playful snowballs, oh what a spree!

Hot cocoa's their secret, warmth in their cups,
While marshmallows dance like cheerful little pups.
They spin stories of pine trees, so proud and so tall,
Enchanting the night with their magical call.

So when winter arrives, with its glistening white,
Listen for laughter, and let your heart light.
For the spirits are near, with each frosty breeze,
Sharing stories, and joy, as they dance through the trees.

Chuckles and Cheery Grins on Frosty Nights

Frosty nights sparkle, with laughter to share,
Snowmen are chuckling, without a single care.
Cheery grins abound, as the moon starts to glow,
While kids in their mittens make snow angels below.

Each snowball a weapon, in a playful fight,
Snowflakes keep swirling, a shimmering sight.
With giggles and shouts, oh the revelry flows,
As frost-covered cheeks get a rosy red glow.

Sledding down hills, it's a wild, joyful ride,
With funny sound effects, we laugh side by side.
While parents sip cocoa, and tell tales of the past,
The chuckles and cheers of the season will last.

So embrace the cold nights, let your laughter take flight,
For the spirit of winter is pure, warm delight.
With chuckles and grins, let your heart feel the cheer,
In this magical season, it's the best time of year.

The Joyful Mischief of Twinkling Eyes

Twinkling eyes peek from behind the soft snow,
Little mischief-makers, in their frosty show.
With sneaky plans brewing, and laughter that bursts,
They scatter the snow, it's a wintery first.

Snowball fights erupt, each throw filled with laughter,
They giggle and scamper, all runnings after.
Chasing their shadows, through the moonlit night,
Creating new memories, oh what pure delight!

They sprinkle the snow with a dash of good cheer,
Building towering forts that shout winter's near.
With cocoa in hand, and a marshmallow way,
Each light-hearted trick turns a night into play.

Oh, the joy in their eyes, with a sparkle so bright,
For mischief's not far on this cold, frosty night.
Join in their fun, let your spirit arise,
For laughter's the treasure, in those twinkling eyes.

The Hidden Giggle of Frosted Pines

In the forest, frosted pines,
Whisper secrets, silly signs.
Squirrels dance in funny suits,
Wearing tiny winter boots.

The branches sway with jolly glee,
As snowflakes shout, "Come laugh with me!"
Each flake a tiny, giggling sprite,
They twirl and spin, oh what a sight!

Trees chuckle with a gentle sway,
While pinecones play their funny play.
Nature's jest, a wobbly rhyme,
In the frosty woods, it's giggle time!

So next time you're beneath the pines,
Listen close for frosty signs.
For laughter hides in nature's cheer,
In every snowflake, joy is near.

Sparkling Joy of the Yuletide Sprites

Yuletide sprites with jolly cheer,
Sprinkle giggles far and near.
They hide in wreaths and twinkle lights,
Bouncing in their frosty flights.

With candy canes and tinsel bright,
They throw a party every night.
Each ornament's a dancing soul,
In this festive, merry scroll.

They giggle on the rooftops high,
As reindeer prance and snowflakes fly.
A joyful chorus fills the air,
With little sprites, beyond compare!

So if you find a jingle bell,
Remember all the tales they tell.
For in every laugh and shining light,
The Yuletide sprites spread pure delight!

A Serenade of Snowflake Laughter

Snowflakes tumble, twist and twirl,
Each one a dancer in a whirl.
They giggle as they touch the ground,
In a symphony of joy profound.

A flurry of faces, a frosty cheer,
As winter whispers, "Come play here!"
They form a blanket, soft and white,
Where every child finds pure delight.

With snowmen laughing, carrots for noses,
And snowball fights, where everyone poses.
A serenade of giggles high,
In this winter wonder, we all fly!

So grab your sled, let laughter soar,
In snowflake laughter, there's always more.
For every flake that falls from grace,
Hides a chuckle, a splendid trace!

Ghosts of Merry Wishes

In the night, with twinkles bright,
Ghosts of wishes take their flight.
They flutter by with playful grins,
Whispering dreams where joy begins.

They sneak through chimneys, soft and light,
Bringing laughter in the night.
Each wish a giggle, every sigh,
A tickle of hope in the moonlit sky.

With every wish, a dance they stake,
Spreading joy like a warm cupcake.
They pull a prank on silent streets,
Leaving footprints in warm sweets.

So if you hear a chuckle near,
The ghosts of wishes have appeared.
Just close your eyes and take a peek,
For laughter secrets, they will speak!

The Radiance of Starlit Playfulness

In the cool of night so bright,
Stars are twinkling, what a sight!
Dancing shadows leap and play,
As moonlight laughs at end of day.

Silly owls in a night parade,
Wearing hats, so unafraid.
The crickets sing a quirky tune,
While raccoons dance beneath the moon.

Chasing dreams on dewy grass,
As fireflies give the best sass.
Laughter echoes with delight,
In the radiance of the night.

So grab your friends and take a chance,
Join the stars in a merry dance!
For in this twilight, fun's the key,
To unlock joy and wild glee!

Enchanted Whispers of Frosty Nights

Beneath the stars' frosty embrace,
Snowflakes waltz, a gentle pace.
Whispers float on chilly air,
As frosty laughter shimmers fair.

A snowman dons a carrot nose,
With googly eyes and frumpy clothes.
While penguins slide on ice so slick,
Waddling fast, oh what a trick!

Mittens stolen, frantic chase,
Frost bites the toes, oh what a race!
Hot cocoa dreams in mugs so bright,
As we share tales by the firelight.

Under blankets, warm and tight,
We giggle soft, till day turns night.
In frosty glee, we find our bliss,
As winter's charm we can't dismiss!

Frost-kissed Dreams in the Twinkle Twilight

In twilight's glow, dreams take flight,
Frost-kissed whispers, soft and light.
Sugarplum fantasies in our head,
As we're bundled warm in comfy bed.

Twirling through a field of snow,
Chasing shadows, watch us go!
Elves in hiding, playing tricks,
As laughter rings in frosty flicks.

Snowmen's hats are blown away,
As playful winds come out to play.
With icy breath and sneaky schemes,
We weave our way through frosty dreams.

In each blink, the stars take shape,
While snowflakes wildly zig and gape.
In this magical, chilly sight,
We find our joy in the twilight.

Echoes of Joy in a Winter Wonderland

In a winter wonderland we roam,
With scarves and hats, we make it home.
Snowball fights and sleds that fly,
Echoes of laughter fill the sky.

The trees wear coats of frosty white,
While nous adorably try to fight!
Through fluffy drifts, we tumble down,
Spreading warmth in a biting town.

As snowflakes dance, the night we chase,
With rosy cheeks, we find our place.
With cocoa hats and marshmallow dreams,
We live our joy in frosty beams.

So find your heart in winter's cheer,
Embrace the magic, hold it dear.
With echoes of joy, we take a stand,
In this snowy, wondrous land!

Radiant Smiles in Frosty Breezes

In winter's chill, we laugh aloud,
While snowflakes dance, we're feeling proud.
The icicles hang like silly jokes,
As frozen fruitcake mocks the folks.

With mittens on, we try to throw,
A snowball that barely makes it, though.
Our noses red, like cherries bright,
We giggle on this frosty night.

The dogs, they prance in fluffy gear,
As they chase sleds that disappear.
A snowman sports a hat askew,
With a carrot nose, that's quite askew.

So raise a cup of cocoa, cheers!
To winter days and silly years.
May every snowman stand up tall,
And every laugh be shared by all.

Faerie Chimes in December's Glow

Amidst the twinkling, bright display,
The faeries like to sing and play.
Their chimes are made of candy canes,
As laughter dances, joy remains.

The gingerbread men march in line,
While frosty mugs scream, 'Drink the wine!'
Each cookie crumb a giggle shared,
In sugary dreams, we all are snared.

With sparkly wings and glittered shoes,
They spread the news of festive views.
As we toast marshmallows on a stick,
Their playful pranks can make you tick!

So join the fun, don't hesitate,
In December's glow, we celebrate.
With faerie chimes and hearts aglow,
Let laughter ring in winter's show!

Frost-kissed Jests and Elusive Sighs

The frosty air brings playful jests,
As we bundle up in our warm vests.
Snowflakes drift, each one unique,
They whisper laughs with every squeak.

The cat in boots, so bold and proud,
Chasing snowballs, he joins the crowd.
While dogs do cartwheels in the snow,
This winter circus puts on a show!

Hot cocoa spills, it's part of the game,
A marshmallow swim, oh such a shame!
With laughter loud, we slip and slide,
On ice that's thin, our joy won't hide.

So here's to frost-kissed jesting cheer,
That warms our hearts, despite the clear.
Let's cherish each silly, frosty sigh,
And dance through winter, you and I!

Merry Echoes Across the Snow

In snowy fields, our laughter rings,
As sleds and snowballs soar on wings.
The echoes bounce on frosty air,
Carried along without a care.

With frosty breath, our jokes take flight,
As winter paints its purest white.
We build a fort, defend our turf,
With snowball cannons, laughs are worth.

The puppies tumble, slip, and slide,
In a magic realm where giggles hide.
A snowman's grin, a perfect mug,
As hot chocolate spills a warming hug.

So gather 'round, let's share a cheer,
To merry echoes far and near.
Through every snowstorm, let it be,
The laughter stays, forever free!

Elusive Smiles Beneath the Starry Veil

In the night sky, giggles swirl,
Stars collect like lost pearls.
A wink from the moon, cheeky and bright,
Whispers tickle the sleepy night.

A comet races with a silly grin,
While aliens dance with a hopeful spin.
Every twinkle's a chuckle, sweet and sly,
Even the owls hoot with a sigh.

Frogs croak poems, frogs in tuxes,
Laughter floats, like curious ducks-es.
The breeze tells tales of mirth once shared,
As the midnight giggles fill the air.

And when dawn breaks, the smiles hide,
In dreams they cackle, far and wide.
Elusive smiles, like shadows they flee,
Beneath the stars, forever carefree.

Winter's Whimsical Embrace

The snowflakes wear hats, nifty and bright,
Snowmen gossip under the moonlight.
Sleds zoom past with squeals of joy,
Taking brave hearts, oh what a ploy!

Hot cocoa simmers, marshmallows dive,
While penguins slide and giggle, alive!
Icicles dangle like frozen mustaches,
As winter's chill brings playful splashes.

Mittens chase mittens, a mismatched game,
Chasing each other, all the same.
A reindeer prances with style and flair,
While frosty breath fills the chilly air.

But as the sun peeks out with a grin,
Winter winks, "Let the fun begin!"
A whimsical hug, so light and breezy,
Leaves us laughing, oh so cheesy!

The Cheer of Glistening Twilight

As twilight drapes its sparkly gown,
The fireflies dance without a frown.
Crickets compose their nighttime jams,
While frogs croak beats to please the clams.

A raccoon dons a dapper mask,
Stealing snacks, what a daring task!
The trees sway gently, checkered with lights,
Whispering secrets about winter nights.

With every gust, the leaves take flight,
Twisting and twirling in sheer delight.
A chipmunk's giggle, a rustling sound,
In the lovely twilight, smiles abound.

So gather round, let's share some cheer,
In glistening twilight, fun is near!
With laughter echoing, soft and bright,
Bathed in the glow of the fading light.

Gladsome Serenades in Snowy Shrouds

Beneath the snow, the critters sing,
In frosty realms, joy's the king.
Squirrels strut in fluffy attire,
Snowflakes twirl, they never tire!

Winter's choir, a jolly tune,
Icicles jingle, morning to noon.
With bundled scarves and rosy cheeks,
The laughter flows, like bubbling creeks.

Hot pies bake in ovens bright,
While kids play tag in pure delight.
Every snowball, a comical shot,
In snowy shrouds, happiness is caught.

So join the dance, be merry and loud,
Amidst the laughter, feel so proud.
For gladsome serenades bloom in the cold,
With warmth and cheer, let the tales unfold.

Winter's Secrets in Giggling Shadows

The snowflakes dance, a giggle parade,
Hiding secrets that winter's made.
Frosty breath joins in the fun,
While snowmen grin beneath the sun.

Icicles hang like playful spears,
Whispers shared in frosty cheers.
Twirls and tumbles, oh what a sight,
In winter's charm, everything's bright.

Sleds fly past, oh what a spree,
Laughter echoes, wild and free.
Hot cocoa waits, a sweet delight,
As winter reveals its secrets tonight.

So grab your mittens, come join the bash,
In giggling shadows, we'll make a splash.

Magical Whirls of Joy and Light

In a twinkling swirl of joyous cheer,
Dancing lights bring the warmth near.
A sprinkle of magic in every flake,
As we glide on the ice, oh what a break!

Jingle bells ring in a wacky tune,
As snowmen try to move to the moon!
Elves on stilts look ready to play,
As laughter drifts like snowflakes away.

The trees are dressed in sparkly garb,
While kids sing loud, not caring if they blurb.
Each moment a whirl, a giddy delight,
In this magical dance of joy and light.

So come join the fun, don't be shy,
With giggles and whirls, let's reach for the sky!

Mirthful Whispers Under Snow-Capped Boughs

Under branches heavy with snowy attire,
Laughter and fun are our heart's desire.
With each soft crunch, secrets softly spill,
Mirthful whispers, bringing us thrill.

Snowflakes tumble, a frosty ballet,
As friends gather round to celebrate play.
Snowball fights break out, oh what a blast,
With giggles that echo, joy unsurpassed.

Hot muffins warm as the cold winds blow,
Cocoa-filled mugs keep spirits aglow.
In cozy corners, we share a tale,
Of snowmen adventures, a frosty trail.

So come take a seat 'neath the boughs so grand,
Mirthful whispers, let's make a stand!

Joyous Hearts Beneath the Mistletoe

Beneath the mistletoe, all bets are off,
Kisses and giggles make everyone scoff.
Silly wishes make the heart flutter,
While friends chuckle loud, oh what a mutter!

With cookies and laughter, we deck the halls,
Prancing around like we're under calls.
Each merry moment is a treasure to hold,
As stories of giggles and wishes unfold.

Twinkling lights brighten every face,
As we chase each other in a joyful race.
Mirthful hearts sing a melody bright,
Under mistletoe's magic, everything's right.

So let's raise a glass to this wondrous glee,
Joyous hearts dancing, forever carefree!

Winterscape of Gleeful Whispers

In a snowy cap, the snowmen smile,
They gather for warmth, in a comical pile.
With carrot noses and eyes made of coal,
They plot mischievous tricks, that's their ultimate goal.

The squirrels in hats trade acorn jokes,
While fashioning sleds from old cardboard folks.
Penguins wear bow ties, glossy and neat,
As they glide on the ice, with silly little feet.

Snowflakes dance down with a giggle and swirl,
As the trees join the fun, in a wintery whirl.
Underneath the bright moon, they twinkle with glee,
Whispering secrets as merry as can be.

From snowball fights, to hot cocoa slips,
The winterscape glimmers with laughter and quips.
As snowmen shake hands and squirrels take flight,
It's a frosty delight, on this magical night.

Laughter by the Hearth in the Stillness

By the crackling fire, warm and bright,
Chirps of laughter fill the night.
With cocoa mustaches and cookies galore,
The kids dream of snowballs, just outside the door.

Grandma tells tales of a yeti so grand,
Who dances and prances, with a band made of sand.
While Grandpa insists he once caught a fish,
That hopped on his plate, granting every wish!

Then suddenly bursts in a cat with a hat,
Sipping hot cocoa, looking oh-so-phat.
He spills all the chocolate, creating a ruckus,
As laughter erupts, joining in the circus.

With each silly story, the warmth fills the air,
We cherish these moments, with love and with care.
In the stillness around, every chuckle does gleam,
By the hearth's laughter, life's a delightful dream.

Revelries in the Mirthful Woods

In the depths of the woods, under tall tree tops,
Critters have gathered, they're dancing like flops.
With rabbits in skirts and foxes in ties,
They sing merry tunes that echo 'neath the skies.

The owls join the party, hooting a beat,
With raccoons juggling nuts, oh what a feat!
A bear in a tutu takes to the floor,
And folks can't stop laughing; they all shout for more!

As pine trees sway gently, they clap their green hands,
The wintery creatures form musical bands.
Snowflakes join in, swirling round the spree,
While squirrels throw glitter, as wild as can be!

When dawn finally breaks, and the moon takes a rest,
The merriment lingers, their hearts feel so blessed.
In the mirthful woods, friendships stick like glue,
With joyous adventures that never feel through!

Joyful Tricks of the Winter Folk

The winter folk gather, with snow in their hair,
Planning their mischief without any care.
From snowballs to pranks that surprise and delight,
They share silly laughs that stretch late into night.

A rabbit with glasses, looks fancy indeed,
While plotting to trip a fast-moving steed.
With carrots for capers, and a snicker or two,
They all scamper off in a whimsical crew.

Frogs wear warm boots, tap dancing on ice,
While owls catch the rhythm, oh isn't it nice?
Hot cider in hand, the forest revels so,
As charming sweet tales of old winter folk glow.

In this joyful world, where laughter runs free,
Mischief and friendship create wonderful glee.
With a pinch of snowflakes and giggles galore,
The tricks of the winter folk, forever we adore!

Mirthful Nightfall in Fairyland

In Fairyland, the jesters play,
With dancing lights that sway and sway.
The mushrooms giggle, fairies prance,
While gnomes attempt a clumsy dance.

The moon is rolling on a hill,
While owls sing tunes with even more thrill.
The stars throw a party, loud and bright,
In this mirthful nightfall, what a sight!

A frog in a top hat starts to croon,
While fireflies join, lighting the gloom.
They make a toast with acorn cups,
And tumble over with wild hiccups.

So if you wander where fairies dwell,
Expect to hear giggles, and all will be well.
For in this world of whimsy and cheer,
Laughter lasts throughout the year.

Secrets Shared 'Neath the Twinkling Sky

Beneath the stars, the secrets flow,
As crickets sing their songs in tow.
The owls are gossiping wise and old,
While raccoons trade stories, bright and bold.

A mouse whispers tales of cheese galore,
While fireflies dance by the dreamy shore.
The moon winks knowingly, oh so sly,
As wishes flutter like clouds passing by.

A unicorn shares her favorite snack,
While fairies giggle, perched on a tack.
They exchange little secrets with fluffy delight,
Under the cover of a starry night.

So gather 'round, let's share a laugh,
As the twinkling sky plays the perfect half.
In this magical space, we sip and share,
The secrets that float through the fragrant air.

Winter's Dance of Jolly Spirits

When winter's chill wraps the world in white,
The spirits giggle, what a delightful sight!
With snowflakes swirling, they spin and glide,
In hats made of cotton and coats of pride.

A snowman winks with a stick for a grin,
While squirrels dash, their cheeks full of win.
They twirl 'round trees, in frostbitten cheer,
As winter's fun draws all spirits near.

The air is filled with laughter and glee,
As snowball fights rage, who will it be?
With puffs of white and shouts all around,
They tumble and roll on the icy ground.

So join the dance in this chilly spree,
Where winter's spirits invite you with glee.
With warm hot cocoa, we'll celebrate,
This jolly time, oh isn't it great?

Tinsel Dreams and Pixie Schemes

In the heart of the night, with tinsel aglow,
Pixies are plotting, with mischief in tow.
They twirl and they swirl, with ribbons of gold,
Creating a tale that never grows old.

With glittering lights, they cover the trees,
Spreading the laughter upon the cool breeze.
The elves join the fun, with bells in their cap,
While snowflakes join in for a whimsical nap.

They sprinkle their dreams with frosty delight,
As wishes float softly into the night.
Their schemes are so silly, their laughter so bright,
Creating a joy that's pure and so right.

So come, take a ride on this tinsel-filled dream,
Where pixies are giggling, or so it would seem.
Under the moonlight, let your cares gleam,
In a world of enchantment, a magical theme.

North Pole Revels Under the Moon

Elves in a snowball fight, oh what a sight,
With cheeks all aglow, they're ready to bite!
Santa's lost his hat, it's stuck on a deer,
'Twas the best of times, full of holiday cheer.

The snowmen are dancing, arms all akimbo,
One slipped on a flake and yelled, "Bingo!"
Rudolph's leading the choir, horns all in tune,
Singing loud praises beneath the bright moon.

Hot cocoa is pouring, marshmallows afloat,
While a penguin in sunglasses reclines in a boat.
Candy canes twirl like they know the routine,
In this polar party, the mood's evergreen.

So raise up your mugs, it's a jolly old show,
As the North Pole revels in winter's sweet glow!
With laughter and joy, our hearts feel alive,
In this winter wonderland, we all can thrive.

Jolly Fables of Twinkling Flights

Once there was a reindeer named Barry McFly,
Who dreamed of the skies, a true aviary guy.
He fashioned himself wings from glitter and glue,
And took to the air, yelling, "Look at me, woo!"

The Christmas lights twinkled, high up in the night,
While Barry zoomed past, eliciting fright.
He crashed through a chimney, oh what a sight!
Gifts scattered like snowflakes, a true starry blight.

Santa was chuckling, "I need a new sleigh,
Or reindeer who don't like to fly into dismay!"
But Barry just laughed, "I'm just feeling so bold!"
As gifts fell like raindrops, all shiny and gold.

So remember dear friends, when things go askew,
Just laugh like dear Barry, and start something new.
For in every mishap, there's a tale to tell,
With jolly old fables that sparkle so well.

Serendipitous Sugary Dances

In a land made of cookies, so crunchy and sweet,
The gingerbread dancers movin' their feet.
Frosting-rimmed legs and candy cane arms,
They boogied and twirled, bringing all kinds of charms.

A marshmallow DJ dropped beats from the sky,
While licorice lasses just danced on by.
Cherries on top swayed to the beat,
As gumdrops skated, nimbly and neat.

Cupcakes in frocks all sparkled so bright,
Inviting the pies for a sugary bite.
Sugar plums giggled, doing the twist,
In this sweet revelry, not a soul was missed.

So if life feels too serious, add sweetness and flair,
Dance like a cookie, float freely in air!
For in every bite of this sugary chance,
Lie the joys of the world, wrapped up in a dance.

Mischief-Makers in the Silent Night

In shadows they whisper, with a glint in their eye,
The little tricksters, as stars fill the sky.
They stealthily sneak through the warmth of the home,
With giggles and snickers, they silently roam.

Mittens on kittens, oh what a sight!
While sugar-hungry vegans could spend a night.
With socks made of tinsel strewn 'cross the floor,
They plotted and planned for even more lore.

A sleigh made of jelly, it wobbles and rocks,
While Peter, the gopher, guards Santa's socks.
In a flash of delight, they all make a dash,
Leaving only confusion and maybe a splash!

So next time you think that the night is so mild,
Remember the laughter of each little child.
For in every quiet, there's mischief and cheer,
In this silent night, let joy be your spear!

The Playful Chime of Crisp Night Air

The night is crisp, the air is bright,
A squirrel dances, what a sight!
He leaps and bounds with no despair,
While I just freeze, a startled hare.

The trees all sway as if they're spry,
The moonlit laughter fills the sky.
But watch your step, there's ice ahead,
Or you'll fall down and bump your head!

The stars up there just wink and wink,
As I attempt to give a clink.
My hot cocoa, it spills with glee,
Just like my hopes of elegance, whee!

So here's to nights so full of cheer,
With playful chimes that bring us near.
We'll laugh and sing 'till morning light,
Then snooze until the next delight!

Harmony of Twinkling Ornaments and Smiles.

The tree stands tall, adorned with cheer,
With ornaments that once were beer!
A family photo on display,
Me at three, my brother's toupee.

We hang the lights, both bright and wild,
As cats pause, suspicious and riled.
A ladder wobbles, oh what a scream!
But who needs safety, when there's gleam!

A garland flops, a tinsel fight,
We twirl and jingle, what a sight!
With smiles wide, we sing off-key,
Who needs a choir? Just you and me!

As snowflakes swirl, we dance and sway,
With laughter ringing through the day.
In this festive, joyful spree,
Ornaments and smiles, our harmony.

Whispers of Frosted Mirth

A frosty wind whispers a tale,
Of snowmen lost, a jolly trail.
Their carrots gone, oh what a crime,
They blame the kids, but it's sublime!

With snowballs flying, laughter's near,
We dodge and weave, let out a cheer.
The dog steals one, he's got no shame,
A fluffy thief in this frosted game.

A mug in hand, it spills with grace,
My tongue's a marshmallow in this race.
We toast to frost in goofy poses,
With every sip, we burst like roses!

So let the mirth continue on,
As winter plays its playful prawn.
With whispers soft and laughter loud,
Let's wrap ourselves in joy, unbowed!

Sparkling Joy Beneath the Stars

Under the stars, we gather round,
With cookies baked and laughter found.
A comet zips, we jump with glee,
But wait, don't grab that last cookie, me!

The milky way, a shiny treat,
While dogs chase fireflies and defeat.
We twirl and spin, our eyes aglow,
Careful of that branch, watch out below!

With friends and marshmallows in sight,
Our campfire crackles, oh what delight!
We tell old tales, both true and tall,
Of ghosts in socks that scared us all!

So here we sit, beneath night's glow,
With sparkling joy that starts to flow.
Each laugh, each smile, a shining star,
Creating memories, near and far!

Gleeful Snowflakes in the Night Breeze

Snowflakes twirl like kids at play,
Dancing down without delay.
They land on noses, coats, and hats,
Making us laugh like silly cats.

One lands square on my dog's head,
He thinks it's time to go to bed.
Rolling in white with great delight,
He's lost his barking; he's taken flight!

Frosty friends in winter's flurry,
Running around, they start to worry.
They tumble down a snowy slope,
Creating chaos, chasing hope.

So let's embrace the chilly cheer,
With frosty hugs, not one ounce of fear.
Gleeful snowflakes, join the jest,
Winter's here, let's have a fest!

Sassy Spirits in the Candlelight

In the flicker of the candle's grin,
Sassy spirits start to spin.
They rustle curtains, tease the air,
Whispering secrets, daring a scare.

One curls up with my mug of tea,
Sipping quietly just to tease me.
They twirl around, what a funky sight,
Mischievous giggles in the night.

They flip the switch on my fridge door,
Giggling at snacks they can explore.
These sassy sprites on a sugar quest,
Stealing treats while I take a rest.

So next time you see a light that's dim,
Know there's a spirit with a wobbly whim.
Candlelit laughter holds the night tight,
Come join the fun, glow with delight!

Whimsies of the Winter Moon

The winter moon with a wink so bright,
Whispers tales of furry delight.
Cats in capes and dogs with hats,
Roaming the night like silly brats.

Snowmen sit, plotting their plays,
Rolling their eyes in snowy bouquets.
They gossip about the frost's great show,
Chasing shadows, putting on a glow.

Elves with snowballs in crafty stance,
Challenge the moon to a winter dance.
With twinkling stars as their stage so grand,
They drift like dreams across the land.

So gather 'round under moon's soft light,
Join the whimsies, take flight tonight.
With laughter echoing, joy's cute rune,
We'll sing to the magic of winter's moon!

Flickers of Joy in the Winter Air

Flickers of joy leap like a spark,
In the brisk air, they leave their mark.
Children squealing on snowy hills,
Catch little dreams mixed with thrills.

Hot cocoa mustache, oh what a sight,
Who knew marshmallows could take a bite?
With giggles and frolic, the fun unfolds,
Winter magic in joy's strong hold.

A snowball fight turns into a dance,
All of us caught in winter's romance.
Laughter rings like chimes in the trees,
As joy flickers softly in the breeze.

So let's bundle up, go out and play,
Chase joy in snow, hip-hip-hooray!
In these chilly moments, hearts will share,
The flickers of joy, beyond compare!

Winks of Winter's Mischief

A snowman danced with glee,
Said, 'Look at me!' with a snowflake hat.
He slipped on ice, oh what a sight,
Fell on his back, like a ragged cat.

The snowball fight began to brew,
With giggles echoing near and far.
But oh, poor Sam got hit anew,
Right in the face—what a bizarre!

Frosty squirrels played peek-a-boo,
Hiding behind the trees so stout.
They laughed and threw their nuts askew,
Winter mischief without a doubt!

So when you see the flakes a-fall,
Remember winter's playful jest.
It might just make you grin and sprawl,
As winks of joy fill up your chest.

Gleeful Spirits at the Hearth

By the fire, the marshmallows pop,
Ghosts do twirl and snicker with cheer.
They roast their tales, and never stop,
With stories that bring a silly fear.

The old cat snores on the mat,
Dreaming of mice in his dainty dreams.
Outside the wind goes 'swoosh' and 'whap',
Inside, it's all giggles and gleams.

Hot cocoa spills, oh what a mess!
The elves are cackling, what a sight!
They toss their hats, feel no stress,
As snowflakes tinkle in pure delight.

So gather 'round and join the fun,
Let laughter echo, crack a grin.
For spirits gleeful, until we're done,
At winter's hearth, let joy begin.

Starlit Giggles in Frosted Glades

Under stars, we skied with flair,
Tripped in snow, our faces aglow.
With every tumble, we'd gasp and stare,
And roll in laughter, all aglow.

An owl hooted, trying to scold,
While mice just chuckled in the night.
A snowflake crown, so pure and bold,
Melts on our heads, what a silly sight!

Frosted trees winked, glam in silver,
As we danced on the ice, oh what fun!
With every slip, our spirits deliver,
Joyful secrets under moonlight's run.

So if you hear a giggle, you see,
Join the fun in frost's playful play.
For starlit nights are wild and free,
With giggles that chase the blues away.

Treetop Secrets and Playful Whispers

In treetops, secrets start to glide,
Woodpeckers whisper, 'Let's play a game!'
Squirrels plotting, with joy they confide,
'Tonight we feast, let's stake our claim!'

They dined on acorns, sweet and crunchy,
Had all the birds vote on their potion.
Feathers rustled, the fun was punchy,
A recipe brewed with sweet devotion.

Beneath the moon, they'd laugh and cheer,
As shadows danced with pure delight.
Unseen by eyes, bringing good cheer,
Treetop wonders, an endless night.

So next time you spot a robin or two,
Listen close, for whispers abound!
The secrets they share are magic, it's true,
In playful mischief, joy can be found.

Starry Wonders and Merry Wonders

The stars above are dancing bright,
They twinkle like they're in a fight.
A comet zooms, just missed a tree,
"Oh dear!" it sighs, "Don't blame me!"

The moon wore shades, so cool and sleek,
He whispered jokes, a bit of cheek.
Constellations, doing the cha-cha,
"Hey, Ursa, where's your dancing partner?"

A shooting star just made a wish,
To turn into a giant fish.
But flopped instead upon the ground,
"Not what I had in mind," it frowned.

Galaxies giggle, swirling fast,
As meteors zip, a cosmic blast.
In this sky, so wild and free,
Who knew the universe loved to be silly?

Winter's Playful Secrets Unveiled

Snowflakes tumble, a frosty dance,
Each one hopes for a quick romance.
A snowman struck a pose so proud,
Until a dog came and barked aloud.

Icicles hang like shy little bells,
Waiting for warmth, they freeze their spells.
"Is it spring yet?" they're all asking,
While winter chuckles, softly basking.

Penguins slide with giggles and glee,
Waddling off to their next cup of tea.
"What's winter without a little chill?"
Said a squirrel with a squirrel-sized thrill.

Hot cocoa's steaming, marshmallows float,
The fireplace crackles, it's truly a goat!
"Jokes on us!" the toys all cheer,
It's winter's playtime, let's spread some cheer!

Laughter Echoes in Cerulean Dreams

In a sky of blue, laughter leaps,
Clouds are pillows where joy softly sleeps.
A seagull sings an off-key tune,
While mermaids dance beneath the moon.

Bubbles rise like giggles in soap,
Floating high, beyond all hope.
"Catch me if you can!" they tease and swirl,
Whirlwinds of fun in a twirling whirl.

Dolphins splash, making a scene,
Wearing sunglasses; they're looking keen.
"Life's a beach!" they squeal with delight,
As the sunset paints the world so bright.

Stars above wink, it's time for play,
"Keep laughing loud to shoo blues away!"
In dreams of cerulean, joy will beam,
As laughter echoes in every dream.

Charm of the Night in Enchanted Glades

In enchanted glades, the fireflies twirl,
Each little light, a dancing pearl.
The owls hoot jokes, wise and sly,
"Who's there?" they tease, as they fly high.

Moonbeams glimmer on the creek,
Whispering secrets they cannot speak.
"I'd fashion a boat," a frog exclaimed,
"On lily pads, I'd be quite famed!"

The trees sway gently, holding hands,
While crickets play in funky bands.
"Even the night has rhythm!" they prance,
As shadows break into a joyful dance.

The breeze brings laughter, light and grand,
While fireflies flicker, a glowing band.
In these glades, where magic weaves,
Charm of the night, oh, how it leaves!

Milton Keynes UK
Ingram Content Group UK Ltd.
UKHW010227111224
452348UK00011B/565